The Blessing of Infidelity
7 Days and 7 Lessons
A Guide through the Darkest Days of an Affair

By Stanley Johnson

ISBN-10: **0692706313**
ISBN-13: **978-0692706312**
Library of Congress Control Number: **2016910821**
LCCN Imprint Name: **Stanley Johnson, Forney, TX**

Dedication

This book is dedicated to my ex-wife and all the women and men who are suffering in silence from infidelity. I know you are trying to navigate life through the darkness of emotional and psychological pain. I believe that you deserve to be loved and cared for the way God intended. I hope that by reading this book, you can find your blessing and your peace to become vulnerable and whole. I hope you can begin the journey, like me, to finding the love for yourself that you deserve. You are not alone. Hopefully I am able to be a light to you as you walk through the terrain of the dark tunnel of infidelity. And I will assure you—because I walked in your shoes—that there is light at the end of the tunnel. I love you and God bless.

Contents

Acknowledgments

As I think about this work and all the people who encouraged me to make this book possible, I can think of many. A few really kept me going, and others have gone to heaven; I would love to share this work with them.

I would be remiss in my duty if I did not acknowledge my Lord and Savior Jesus the Christ for His strength and guidance through the power of the Holy Spirit that has kept me diligently fighting to focus on my assignment. I also want to thank my wife for having the strength to leave me. Had you not left me, I know this book would not exist. You are strong, and I hope nothing but the best for you. I want to thank my father, Samuel Johnson Sr., for giving me a place to turn when I lost my way. I am so grateful. I know you did your best to raise my siblings and me to be great women and men for God. I wish you were here so I could tell you that you did it.

I want to thank my mother, Ozell Mitchell-Johnson-Brumfield. I miss you so much. I would love for you to share this momentous challenge with me. Your love and the principles of grace that you displayed throughout my life have become a stepping-stone for me into the peace I have in my life. I love you.

I also want to thank my "baby," Lucille Johnson. Woman, you have been my rock. I love you so much. You mean the world to me. Words cannot explain the love that I have for you. You are my sister by blood, my prophet and counselor by Christian experience, and my ear by being my friend. Thank you for being my ear.

I also want to acknowledge Michelle Grady-Cathcart. You are a real friend. I know God sent you into my life for this season. Thank you for your advice and your prayers.

I want to acknowledge Andrea Perry. You are a friend indeed. God has used you as a minister of love toward me. I really appreciate you. You haven't judged me; you put yourself in my shoes. I really appreciate you for doing that. I really value our friendship and the ministry you gave to me during this process.

I want to thank my sister Lorraine Johnson for picking up the phone when I needed to talk in the beginning of this process. I really value and appreciate you.

Michael Knighton, thanks for calling and checking on me. It seemed that God was using you when I needed someone to talk to the most. Thanks for being obedient to God and reaching out to me. Love you for that!

Finally, I will be always grateful to the Meier Clinic. Thank God for my counselor, John. I thank God for using you to guide me into a direction of hope and peace. I am indebted to you for my life.

I have not mentioned many of you who have given me the strength to keep on writing. You all believed that God gave me this assignment and work. To all of you, I thank you. I appreciate you for being sensitive to God's call and believing in me.

To all of you reading this statement, I am proud of you for searching for answers. I hope this book ministers to you and gives you some direction to make it through to a brighter day. Thanks for your support. God bless.

Introduction

I cheated on my wife for twenty years. I knew it was wrong, but I could not seem to stop. I chalked it up to just being a man, but deep down inside I really did not want to be the type of man who was cheating on his wife.

The Bible talks about how the only temptations that get us to participate in them are the ones most common to us. But God is faithful to us—so much so that He will not allow us to be tempted beyond that which we are able to resist, but He will use the same type of temptation that we keep making the mistakes with to break the habit of the temptation (1 Cor. 10:13). If this scripture ever came to life, it came to life on June 1, 2014.

On this day, I found out that my wife was having an affair. God allowed me to feel the pain I was inflicting on my wife. This is why this verse resonates with me.

I was mad, angry, and whatever other words you can think of. I was not thinking about the infidelity as a message from God as I see now. It was one of the most emotionally painful moments of my life. However, as I was able to gain composure, I began to see the blessing in the infidelity.

This book is not a platform for me to defame my wife's character or to blow off steam. However, as I am on my journey to mental, spiritual, and physical health, I wanted to share my experience with people who are dealing with infidelity and are looking for answers. Perhaps at some time or another we all have seen people who want to send some type of message to a violating spouse, partner, or fiancé that hurting them is a precursor for retaliation. Based on my experience, acting out in this way actually is a cry for attention and support.

This book is about healthy emotional healing. I wrote this book for the person who is trying to understand "What the *hell* just happened?" You may be reading this book with a sense and feeling of "Why am I going through this?" Well, you have found the right book, and you are asking the right questions. I am going to share my experience of how God, my wife, and psychotherapy gave me meaning and purpose to my "why" questions, to my life, and the seven lessons I learned over seven days.

I am going to walk you through my first seven days of pure heartbreak and confusion. I wouldn't wish this experience on my worst enemy. I hope to be as descriptive as possible. I want you to hear my heart beat through this project. I hope to paint a picture of how empty love can sound. I hope to color the canvas of my experience so that you can hear and see what infidelity can do to a relationship and to a person. I want you to hear the crackling in the mattress as I attempt to get comfortable. I want you to see the rolling tears on my pillow as I talk softly to God and as a trickle of moonlight squeezes ever so gently through my window. I want you to hear the anguish in my voice as it trembled and shuddered when she left me alone, and all I could ask her was, "Why?" I want to show you how I found solutions in this moment.

The First Seven Days and Seven Life Lessons

If there was anything that challenged me in life, it was my first seven days. Here is my belief: "If you can make it through the first seven days, then you will make it through to peace and contentment." I think the reason it was the hardest was that I did not know what to do. It was something that came "all of a sudden!" It was that "bam, in your face" type of thing, and it sent me into a world of confusion. I am sure if you are dealing with finding out about an affair, you are trying to find answers. I want to give a list of life lessons.

What I envision for you to receive from this book is a deeper meaning of life and love. I know that may be hard to see because you are angry, and you are really trying to focus on finding comfort from this affair. But trust me—as the days go on, you will probably come back to this book and read it again. You will get better. I also want you to identify God in this. Yes, God. Our life partners were really looking for God's love. When we truly understand God's love, we have to point to Christ. The Bible says, "While we were yet in sin, Christ died for us" (Rom. 5:8). The Bible also says, "God so loved the world that He gave His only begotten Son that whosoever believes in Him should not perish, but have everlasting life" (John 3:16). These verses of scripture define God's love as sacrificial. This means that when God shows us love, He shows it to us through acts of sacrifice. This means that if we are going to follow the example of God, we should love our life partners through acts of sacrifice.

Ask yourself this question: "Was I giving my life partner love sacrificially?" If reconciled, what are you willing to sacrifice to make sure you honor your life partner with your time and attention? God's love toward us is the sure way to respond to these questions. We should love our life partners as our heavenly Father loves us. God's love is full of grace and mercy. His love is not judgmental. God's love is not self-serving. But His love is patient and considerate. He wants us to enjoy a life full of His love and commitment to us. Did you give this type of love to your life partner?

I want to thank God for the blessing of infidelity. I did not think God would use infidelity to push me into my purpose. I hate that He had to do it. But I am so glad He did. I guess the best way to describe it is "I feel free." I don't have to lie and deceive anymore. Infidelity is one of the most ego-killing things that a man or woman can do to a life partner. I can now speak from both sides of the experience.

When God's got a call on your life, He does not care about a man's or a woman's ego. He wants to give us something that is real. You see, we must put Him first in our lives, including in our relationships. God wants to be first. Is God first in your life or in your relationship? I want to share with you how He taught me how to put Him first. God wants us to get rid of the substitutes and to put Him first! I am so committed to supporting my wife's emotional and psychological healing. I love her, and I still would like to be with her. I know the title might come across as invasive and negative, but I have a call to answer.

Secrecy and deception destroy relationships. I think true

healing is when you and I can be transparent and let the world know that we all have problems and that we are willing to be vulnerable and not care about what people think of us. Jesus died on Calvary to bring us healing and support regardless of our past and present sins. His love was an example to every believer that, regardless of life challenges, God's grace and mercy are available to us.

As I look back on these seven days, I am able to identify the type of love I was giving to my wife as I now compare it to the love of God. I want to share with you how God "set me up for the help I needed" to finally push me to the change I desired. I am going to talk to you about that in this book so you can possibly start identifying your "setup moment." This is the moment when you can identify God in your situation.

I also want you to be able to find peace and courage to get your composure and focus back. As you explore my first seven days, I want you to gain some insight about how to proceed with your life from whatever point you learned about the infidelity. So, let's get started!

The Setup

I feel it's important to tell you about the day before I got the heartbreaking news of the affair. I think God prepared my heart for the blow I was going to be receiving on June 1, 2014.

As I look back on that day, I exhibited a great calm when I learned that my wife was having an affair. My calmness came off as if the news were something I expected. It was as if someone slapped me hard in the face, and I stood there as if nothing had happened. But it was God's plan. He prepared my heart to receive the news. He set me up.

I Was Ready for Change

The day before the affair was May 31, 2014. I had to work an event that night, so I spent my day prepping for it. I am an event photographer. The Dallas African American Museum hired me to photograph their gala and fund-raiser. I also had another event at the Shark Bar, a local nightclub in Plano, Texas, afterward.

I don't know what it was, but that night I had a strong sense and desire for more out of life. I was drained. I felt like I was working to be working. It was unfulfilling, and I did not like it because I felt empty. This night I was determined to go after the change I wanted. I was at a point that I wanted God. I was tired of running from Him.

I also wanted to love my wife properly. I really was ready to give my all to her because I really felt she deserved it. My wife and I had been together at that time for twenty years, and I can't remember a year when I was faithful. This passion for God and desire to change caused me to call my wife and tell her that I was going to be shutting down early, and I was coming home.

She replied to me, "Come on home, baby." The sound of her voice heightened my desire to get home to her. She asked me to pick up some Taco Bell on my way. Wow, I was excited because I wanted us to start all over again. I could see it. However, while I was driving, I had a strong desire to pray. As I was praying, I ask God to help me to change. I was tired. I wanted peace in my life. I was never faithful to my wife, and this reality haunted me. I had known something was wrong psychologically for a long time, but I was trying to solve my own problems.

I picked up my wife's Taco Bell order and headed home. As I was turning the corner to my street, I began to cry uncontrollably. I could actually hear the tapping sound of my tears hitting the crotch of my pants. The tears were just rolling down my face. As I look back at this moment, I see it as the time God started the process of my change. This is the point when He had confirmed my readiness for change. I must have sat in my van for about thirty minutes praying and crying.

I finally got a grip on myself and was able to turn my van off and head into my home. When I walked through the door, I went to my wife's side of the bed, handed her the Taco Bell order, and kissed her. I had not been able to do this for almost a year. It felt strange. I had so much guilt and shame.

Guilt and shame will eat at your heart like a cancer and draw out of you an emotionally debilitating depression. I think God uses these emotions to signal our need for change and our need for Him. I also was ready to change for my wife. I wanted to give her the love that she deserved. One of the changes I desired was to start going to church again. I had already made up my mind that I was not going to make any excuses. I was going to church with or without my wife. But what happened the next day exposed a deeper change that I needed. It was a deeper change that I ignored.

The next seven days of challenge I hope will help a young man or woman navigate the up-and-down roller coaster that is hard to get off once the infidelity is disclosed. I want to give you some life lessons that perhaps will bless you. This is my GPS system to help you identify the deeper change that you really need in your life as you journey past the pain of infidelity.

Your spouse's infidelity is not by accident. It is a message that God is sending to you about the deeper change that you need in your life.

Chapter 1
Day 1-Life Lesson 1
Listening Loud and Clear

She yelled at me from the top of her lungs, "F—k you!" And in another frail and hurting breath, she said, "You did this, Stanley!" This is what my wife told me after I got a message on Facebook from a young woman hurt over finding my wife and her boyfriend in bed together. But my morning did not start with that drama.

I woke up out of what I considered an incredible dream. I was with my wife on a beach. I know it was a private or remote location because it was just her and me, kissing and making out to the sound of crashing waves beating against the shore. We were rolling in the sand, kissing, and touching each other ever so gently. I remember kissing her lips in the dream and telling her how much I loved her. And then I woke from my sleep only to find her sleeping on her back, her head sunken into the pillow. Man, she looked like a princess. Just looking at her aroused me. I started kissing and touching her. I felt a little resistance, but I ignored it. We made love. We lay talking for about an hour, and then I said to her, "Baby, let's get up and get dressed because we are going to church." She got up and started to get dressed.

As my wife was combing her hair in the bathroom mirror, she and I talked about a new start. Then, all of a sudden, I got an inbox message from Facebook that read:

> Hello…I sent you a message yesterday on your Facebook page. I found your wife in bed with my man last night. She was also with him last week in New Orleans from what I understand. When I realized that she was married, I thought her husband should know. I am obviously hurt, and she has ruined my relationship. I asked [my boyfriend] if he knew she was married and if she knew he was involved with me. He admitted they both knew and blamed it on lust. Just as she told me last night, after she got dressed, "I, too, am sorry that you have an unfaithful partner, and this is a messed up situation."

My heart started beating one hundred miles an hour, the light in the house became dim, and—for some strange reason—I could not breathe. The only question I could ask was why.

But I knew why. You see, for years I had developed a hearing system with my wife and not a listening one. But on this day, I listened to her loud and clear. I listened to three things. First, she had felt alone for years. Second, she was no longer the seventeen-year-old girl I had met in college. She did not need my protection anymore. Finally, I was the cause of all of the mess. Had I paid her attention, she suggested, I would not be going through the pain of finding out about the affair.

Let me be clear—I take full responsibility for all my actions in this relationship. But I now notice one thing in this moment, as I am removed from this day and able to see it for what it was. I couldn't make her do anything; she had to take responsibility for that. But what I can say is that she deserved to be treated with respect, love, and attention, and I did not give her that. This woman was by herself for years. She was alone in a marriage. I think if I had been alone, I would have been in a state of vulnerability.

Alone (Her Reality and Feeling Alone)

Her eyes opened, her face turned red, she inhaled, and what came out was molten fire. It was like a volcano that had been waiting to erupt. Erupt she did. With tears rolling down her face, she explained to me that she hated being in the house by herself. She told me about things she held back because she did not want to lose our relationship. Her face was a mixture of pain and liberation.

She made one of the most profound statements about her growth that I missed. She said, "I am no longer the seventeen-year-old girl you met at Nicholls State University." She finished her statement by saying, "I am a woman!"

Wow, I look at this as a statement of liberation for her. I could feel it when she said it. This statement produced a silence that made me feel as if I had duct tape over my mouth. I could finally listen to her. Man, it was loud, it was true, and it was real—for me especially.

She looked free. Yes, free. Free from the darkness of asking me for my time. Free from the need for me to fulfill her needs. She wanted freedom. She wanted to be loved on her terms. She spoke her own love language, and I finally listened to her voice.

She was declaring her independence, and she did not care if I liked it. Yes. She spoke loud and clear, and for the first time in a long time, I listened to her. I finally got it. She gave me a life lesson that has changed me and changed my perception of old male chauvinistic fallacies that I got from my father. Don't get me wrong; my father did his best to instill in me a sense of manhood and responsibility to my family. The realization of this moment showed me that there was something missing.

Life Lesson

The life lesson I took from this moment was that when a life partner is asking for our time, he or she is really crying for love and attention. The partner is feeling alone. He or she is not asking for time only. The partner is asking to be understood. The partner has a need to be recognized amid the hustle and bustle of our lives. The person wants to talk and to be listened to. I didn't get this then, but I get it now. I want to take this time to affirm my now ex-wife. Sweetheart, thank you. If you have found love somewhere else, I am happy for you. However, thanks for the lesson and the blessing of leaving me. I really needed this time to find "me." Thank you for speaking this message loud and clear.

"I Am a Woman!"

"I am not the seventeen-year-old girl you met in college, Stanley," she said while crying and screaming at the top of lungs. "I gave you all of me, not some of me." She wanted me to understand that her affair was not about her needing a man. She was really crying out for me. I believe she realized what she had done. She hated that all that we went through led to an affair.

I had taken her for granted. I had never stopped to see her growth. I had never understood her loneliness. My wife had been lonely, and I had heard her and did not care. All I seemed to be concerned about was making money. I kept her in a locked box. But I did not realize that she had broken from it. She was so strong. For four years, she was at home and alone.

She used to tell me about parties, and I would ignore them. She planned a trip that she invested $3,000 in, and I treated it as if it interfered with my making money. For her birthday in 2013, I did nothing. I was lost and in a trance after money. My wife's affair snapped me out of it. For me, my wife's affair was like the burning bush was for Moses. It got my attention.

The Bible speaks about how God used a burning bush to get Moses's attention to talk to him about delivering the children of Israel from Egyptian bondage (Exod. 3). When God got Moses's attention, He was able to give him the assignment to set the children of Israel free. Well, infidelity was my burning bush, and this book is one of my assignments God gave me for people who are looking for answers and feel like they don't have a way out of the bondage of infidelity. It made me realize where I was, who I had become, and what I needed to do. I realized at that time that I needed help. Yes. Hard as it was to accept this affair, it saved my life. Looking back on this day, this was God's answer to my prayer from the previous night sitting in my van. God had heard me and listened to me. I did not see it then, but I see it now. God used the pain that I was inflicting on my wife to deliver me. He literally stepped in and said, "Enough!"

And I said, "I agree!"

My wife claiming her independence by stating to me that she was a woman reminds me of the movie *The Color Purple* where the character of Sophia, played by Oprah Winfrey, one of the most recognized persons on television, says to Celie, played by Whoopi Goldberg after getting married to Harpo, "I's a woman now, Miss Celie." Sophia wanted Miss Celie to recognize her womanhood. In the same way, my wife's womanhood was revealed. I noticed it.

Yes. I noticed it. She was a woman.

Independence is a powerful message and declaration. It can either cause war or peace. I was tired of war. I wanted peace. Her liberation opened my eyes to the peace I needed inwardly. My wife claiming her womanhood, and owning it was both amazing and confusing at the same time. Her claiming her independence was amazing because I had never seen my wife in this light. She was ready to take care of herself. She was ready to set her own path. And she was ready to go through life alone instead of putting up with my mess. This confused me because I had never noticed this woman. Wow. She was sexy. She was beautiful. If I had never seen womanhood being expressed, I saw it in my wife on that day.

Life Lesson

The life lesson I received from this declaration of independence was that she really didn't need me. I think that's it. If I had loved my wife from a perspective that she really didn't need me, I would have been more aware of her growth and development. I can say that because when she declared her independence, I was able to see her growth. If you are in a relationship where you feel you are not viewed as evolving and growing, then it may be time for you to declare your independence. There is an old saying: "You can do bad all by yourself!"

"You Did This to Us"

My wife said, "You did this to us!"

"Really," I thought when I heard this. I was like, "Oh, it was me…" I was still selfish and self-centered. I didn't realize it then. But I realize it now. I am writing this book about four months out from the time the affair was revealed, so I can clearly see where I share some of the blame for my wife's affair.

I was making that money, or so I thought. However, the Bible says, "The love of money is the root of all evil" (1 Tim. 6:10). I think the Bible was describing my passion behind it. I loved it! I ignored my wife for it. I fulfilled my personal indiscretions with it.

It came across as an answer to all my problems. But it was all a lie. My wife was not cheating on me. She wanted to feel like a woman. She wanted to be loved. She wanted me to compliment her and affirm her. I was so caught up in "making that money" that I ignored the need she wanted me to fulfill in her life. I was assuming that buying her things was fulfilling her needs. She proved me wrong. She didn't care about money. She wanted me.

How It All Happened

She had asked me a year before to go with her to her class reunion. I put her off. I loved that money. She got two of her friends to go with her. While at the reunion, a young man approached her. My wife explained to me in a conversation that her lover mentioned to her how beautiful she was. He was attracted to her. He made her feel like a woman. He did not ignore her womanhood. He complimented it. He gave her a feeling that was different from what I was giving her. He was giving her time and attention. This was a hard life lesson for me.

If you are reading this book and your wife or husband is having an affair, part of the blame for the affair has your name on it. The easy thing to do is to focus on what he or she has done. You see, that's the selfish side of us. I was talking to someone recently, and I was explaining that this affair allowed me to see the reflection of my behavior. This was, in essence, what I call **my mirror-effect moment.**

My Mirror-Effect Moment

My mirror-effect moment was the moment I realized the reflection of my behavior in the mirror of life and the consequences that come with it. That is, what I was going through was a reflection and the consequence of my behavior. It is actually a good moment. The love of money, sex, and power was a vicious drug for me. I was an addict, and I never stopped chasing my high.

This affair wrapped its arms around me as a wrestler would to take down his or her opponent. It put me in a headlock and forced me in front of the mirror of life to see the effects of my addiction.

The lie I was telling myself was that I was OK. I was not OK. I was out of control and hurting. I was living with guilt and shame. I was afraid, and I needed God, but I put Him last in my life.

The mirror of life does not lie. It's like any other mirror. That is, "What you see is what you get." So, what do I do now? I decided to change what I was looking at in the mirror. I knew the change I needed was not going to occur overnight. And I accepted the time it was going to take to change into the man I desired to be.

Change What I See? Or See the Change I Desired?

I chose to change what I saw. I got a look into the mirror of life, and I hated what I had become. I had turned into a selfish, self-centered, money-chasing, immoral creature who did not deserve to be leading anybody's life or be in someone's life. Had I chosen to see my change, I would have chosen to fix myself. Hell no! I did not need a choice! I needed a change. But I knew that to change what I knew would take some time and some effort. I had already damaged my relationship, and this blow to our relationship could only mean separation or divorce; asking my wife to wait for me to get help was out of the question.

I started trying to find help. Guess who came to my rescue? My wife came to my rescue. Yes. She told me about the Meier Clinic. Her cousin had gone there for help, and they helped her. I am so glad I found the Meier Clinic.

I needed answers and got all the answers I needed. Guess whose insurance supported my help? Yes. My wife's health insurance supported the help I needed. I hope by this time, you are beginning to see how God strategically put me with this woman to help me navigate through not only the pain of the affair but the pain of my past. So even if we do not make it through this affair, and we go our separate ways, I am going to forever be in debt to her.

My journey was secured. I had to change not just for this relationship, but for me and for God.

Life Lesson

The life lesson I got from this was that sometimes God puts us with people, in places, or with things to navigate us into our greater purpose in the universe. It may come across that we are hurting, but life is sending us a message of hope that points us in the direction of the journey God wants us on. Life sometimes gives us temporary setbacks to give us long-term success.

Chapter 2
Day 2-Life Lesson 2
The Boost I Needed for Change

This affair was definitely my holy grail for change. Yes. I needed to refocus my attention on what was more important. I wanted a plan that included love for me and my family. I was so caught up with money, all the fun I thought I was having, and all the success I thought I was experiencing that I put myself and my family on the back burner.

When I began to examine myself, I realized that I needed God's direction. I needed to give my wife proper love. I could have focused all my attention on what my wife had done, but that would have been too easy. The bigger challenge for me was to focus my energy on me and what I needed to change about myself. I did not want to continue my life cheating on my wife and living with the guilt and shame.

I felt that God at this time had answered my prayers. The only thing I wondered about was what to do about my relationship.

I decided to do three things. First, I started digging deep within myself. I always knew that something was wrong psychologically. I always needed help, but I thought I could just trust God and everything would be OK. Second, I realized that I needed to become self-aware. I talked about looking into the mirror of life. This is where I began to see who I really had become, and how what happened was as a result of my behavior. And finally, I wanted to claim the man I desired to be for God, my family, and myself. God has a purpose for my life. I wanted more out of life and for my family. I didn't want to keep living a life of constant affairs.

Digging Deep

I was scrambling around on the second day, trying to do whatever I thought would bring normal back. Little did I know that normal was far away. I wanted to change, but at first I was trying to fix the situation. What I did not realize was I was trying to fix a situation only God and time could repair. The damage I caused had resulted in and produced relationship destruction and emotional pain. I had no other choice but to turn to God.

I had realized that my wife's lover made her feel beautiful. He may have given her the confidence she needed to leave our marriage. He rescued her from a relationship where she was left alone. She perhaps felt unattractive and unappreciated. He was her new love interest. I was the bad guy. I had pushed her into another man's arms. This realization was what I needed to change. I needed to dig deep. The change I needed was not a surface change. I needed something deeper.

I reached out to the Meier Clinic to dig deeper. The Meier Clinic is a Christian-based counseling center for believers. Yes, me. I wanted God, His angels, Joseph, and Mary to come to my home and fix my marriage. But it was not the marriage that needed to be fixed. It was me. I needed a deep cleansing. It was like a mechanic's hands at a nail salon. I required a little extra help and attention. It was like one of the characters on the hit TV series, *Martin.* I felt like I had "Myra's feet." This character's feet were so jacked up that Sheneneh said, "When you do Myra's feet, you gotta go to work."

You see, I needed special attention because the old emotional wounds and issues that stemmed from my childhood had surfaced. I needed to get answers to deep-seated issues that went unresolved.

Life Lesson

So the life lesson I took from this was that sometimes the problems that surface in our relationship are unresolved pains and issues from our past. Paying attention to patterns will reveal to you the deep-rooted issues that are affecting your current relationships. Get help! You cannot do it on your own. You need to get help so you can go deep into your past to start the process of healing from those things.

I Needed to Become Self-Aware

What does self-awareness mean? Self-awareness is when we are living in the present and are able to identify the reality of what's going on around us. I was very unaware of my identity, my relationship, and my desires. I allowed money, people, and places to affect my view of reality.

I was poor. I had never had anything. To make the kind of money I was making was destructive for me. I had a belief system that was nurtured in dysfunction. Money meant cars, clothing, fun, and material things. I put money away, but I blew most of it. When I became self-aware, I became receptive to the idea that I was lost and out of control; having access to the money I was making contributed, big time, to my behavior.

In reality, I was battling loneliness, depression, and emotional pain. I was too ashamed to ask for help because I had built up this image that I had everything together.

Life Lesson

The life lesson I gained from this affair regarding self-awareness was that asking for help is OK. Perhaps you are reading this book and possibly may relate to living a life that gives you access to things that shield your pain, your depression, your fears, and your anxieties. You are not alone. You can get help. Call the Meier Clinic. Call a close friend. Call somebody. Get in touch with reality. You need help. Your life is out of control. You cannot fix it. You messed it up. Let a professional help you get to the root of your problem to start fixing it. It's not until you are able to do this that you will find the peace that you are seeking. This is not about the affair. It is about you now. I found my peace. It was in the hands of God, my therapist, and my support team.

Once I was able to accept that I was out of control, I began to seek help. Don't be like me. Get help now while you can still save your relationship. It is time to live in the now. Tomorrow is not promised to you. Your past is over. Do something today. Stop reading this book and get the reality check you need. I love you.

God loves you. And if you love yourself and the people your behavior has hurt, you will get the help you need. Look into the mirror of life. It's calling for you to change.

I Want to Be the Man I Always Desired to Be

I never wanted to be a self-centered and selfish butt crack. I wondered for many years, "Lord, how did I get to this?" I had lost all sense of direction. After Hurricane Katrina, I was angry. I was depressed. I was empty. I had to start all over again. I hated it. I think the devil needed this fuel to start working on his destructive plan for me.

The Bible says that the "enemy comes to steal, to kill, and to destroy" (John 10:10). I truly can say that was the devil's plan for me. He wanted to steal my identity. He wanted to put a label on me associated with a person I never wanted to become. He also wanted to kill everything that was bringing me joy and happiness. He came after my marriage, my health, and my career. Finally, he wanted to wipe me clean off the planet. I was a threat. The devil saw something in me that he has seen in life impactors like Jesus, Moses, Elijah, Oprah, Malcolm X, and so on. He knew my potential. And he knew if I continued trusting God the way I had before the storm, I would affect many. Don't let the devil stop you from being the man or woman you truly desire to be.

Don't Let the Devil Ultimately Destroy Who You Are

Yes. The devil knows he can't kill you because God won't let him. So his next tactic is to steal from you. The devil's ultimate goal is to destroy you by stealing from you. I would assume the devil thinks that your love for life, yourself, and God is tied to possessions. And he knows that those of us who do not love ourselves are prone to be connected emotionally to things that are in our possession. So he tries to steal from us.

So I pose the question: What is it about you and me that the devil is trying to steal from us to destroy us?

The first answer is that you are a child of God. The second answer is that you have talents and gifts from God that God wants to use in the universe. The third answer is God is using the affair as a warning signal to you. You had probably gotten a warning before and ignored it. So I believe God is using this book to send it again. This is so you can get back in line to your call and purpose. God plans to make you a contributor to the universe, and the devil doesn't like it.

The Devil's Ultimate Goal

The devil's ultimate goal is to get us into a situation where we start trusting in ourselves. He uses this method because he knows what a life dedicated to God looks like. And on the other hand, he knows what a life that lack's God's guidance looks like. A life that lacks God's guidance is filled with self-inflicted consequences. He doesn't want us to trust God. He doesn't want us to seek God for answers in our relationships. He knows that once we start trusting in our abilities, he can infiltrate our minds and manipulate us to inflict pain on ourselves.

Life Lesson

The life lesson I learned on Day 2 was the reality that the preoccupations in our lives pull us away from the reality of the valuable and important things being taken out of our lives. It's time to become self-aware and get help.

Chapter 3
Day 3-Life Lesson 3
Tables Have Turned

When the tables turned on me, I soon realized that life also changed. It seemed that the woman whom I had left alone for four and a half years was feeling liberated. She was free, and she was wearing freedom well. You see, I had had repeated affairs before and during my marriage. When I got a taste of the bitter medicine of infidelity, I vomited to its taste as I had to the spoonful of castor oil my dad gave me every winter as a child. It was nasty. I thought I was going to pass out. I was light-headed. But in the midst of all these emotions, I realized that this was what my wife had to endure to get past my behavior. It opened my eyes.

Life Lesson

I took three life lessons from this day. First, my wife deserved to be loved in the correct way. I was giving my wife the love my mother endured from my father. I hated the way he treated her. This is how blinded I was.

Second, I now had to endure the loneliness she felt for four and a half years. She left the house. She was now sleeping out. Guess where? She was now sleeping with her lover.

Finally, I had to accept that the woman I took for granted all these years had now been changed.

My Wife Deserved the Correct Love

How do you give a person the correct kind of love? The best way to explain it is in the statements of Jesus Christ when He said that the greatest commandments to follow are the first two laws of the Ten Commandments. That is, we should love the Lord God with all of our hearts, with all of our minds, with all of our souls, and with all of our strength. Then He said, "The second is like unto the first...Love your neighbor as yourself" (Mark 12:31). I lost touch with this. I was so selfish and self-centered that I totally lost my way. I had abandoned my love for God. I had used my heart to love money. I used my strength to chase it. Making money was all I thought about. I had sold my soul to the idea of making money so much so that nothing else mattered. Had I given my wife the love that God wants us to exhibit to others, perhaps my wife would have never had the affair.

The affair was like a distress flare from a ship stranded at sea. It was my wife's way and God's way of saying, "Hey, over here…we need help!"

I was so selfish and self-centered that my attitude was like, "I don't care about you being stranded."

You see, the lover saw the flare and answered the distress call. You and I have to keep in mind that the lover is not the true help your wife or husband wanted. The lover is just responding to a call that you and I ignored. In fact, it may even seem like it is too late.

But now is the time to provide the correct love he or she deserves. We couldn't do it when we were with them. So, do it now that you are away. Love him or her like you want her to be loved. In my case, I want to love my wife the same way I wanted to be loved after she discovered all of my affairs. This is the perfect time to treat your wife the way you want to be treated.

Life Lesson

The life lesson I took from this day was that I needed boundaries to protect my love, not only for my wife but also for myself. I had to "man up" to accept the consequences of my ignorance. Here is my advice to you. It's time to start setting boundaries in your life. If you don't know how, get help; it's time to learn.

If you have access, get online and "Google it." Go to the library and check out books on *setting boundaries in relationships*! God wants all of your heart, your mind, your soul, and your strength. Your wife or husband is no different. When a person has boundaries, he or she can love with all his or her heart, mind, soul, and strength!

This is why the loneliness was so brutal to me. It felt like I was in a dark hole. I soon realized that loneliness was the price of taking a person for granted. I learned in therapy that my brain had registered my wife as a source of love, and now that she is gone, it craves her.

This is why you and I are going through the pain of loss and loneliness. I got that from my therapist, too. Keep in mind that my wife had changed. She had changed and didn't update me. Why? I never took the time to check in on that.

Loneliness Is Brutal

I had been with my wife for twenty years, so to be home without her was brutal. The emptiness in silence can be all-out dangerous. I did not want to commit suicide, but I hated this feeling of emptiness. It was so dark. It gripped me in its clutches and would not let me go. It was like the boa constrictor that slowly kills its prey by squeezing the life out of it.

Loneliness had wrapped me in its deadly coil; the more I moved, the tighter the loneliness became. It also suffocated me.

I remember lying in bed, tossing and turning. The mattress crackled like an empty plastic bag. Everything seemed dark and empty. Then it hit me. This is what she must have felt all those years being confined to our toxic relationship. You see, the tables had turned.

For years she had asked me for my time and affection. I have to say, this was my third day, and I could not handle it. Imagine, for four and a half years she did what I was now experiencing. Man, she is a strong woman.

This was not a time for me to want her back. This was a time for me to experience the pain she had experienced. I didn't like it! This is why you must remember this feeling of loneliness if you and your wife or husband get back together or if you get into a new relationship.

Life Lesson

This life lesson gave me the blessing of loneliness. I don't wish it on my worst enemy. The next relationship I explore will be blessed with this understanding. I realized that a boa constrictor called loneliness squeezed my wife, and it killed all the love she had for me. She even told me that she loved me, but she was not in love with me. I know now what that meant. What that meant to me was the woman I knew was gone. The relationship was gone. The intimate love that she had in her heart for me was gone. This is why I say that loneliness is brutal.

Loneliness hit me in so many places that it left me emotionally sore. It's like the pain that flu patients experience. The pain of the flu is felt all over your body. Loneliness will leave you with deep bruises that only God, time, and professional help can heal.

My Wife Changed and I Didn't Expect Her To

She sat down on this day and made a list of times that I cheated on her. She chronicled those from the time we met until 2014. Based on her list, it seemed every year that we were together I had an affair.

This may not be your situation. But whatever drove your wife or husband into a lover's arms, trust me—you had something to do with it. You took him or her for granted. You thought your sex, or your money, or your success was enough. Our life partners deserve respect. Oh, I will listen now.

If I get into another relationship—or if my wife and I get back together—I will definitely give my life partner the gift of listening and responding appropriately.

I Took My Wife for Granted

I took my wife for granted. I used to tell her stuff like, "You aren't going anywhere." This statement alone said how I felt about my relationship. It said I wanted control. I wanted things my way, and I didn't care if she agreed. This is toxic. You think our wives and husbands want to be with their lovers? No. The lover is a substitute for us. When you think about that, the lover is being used. Our life partners really want us. But they are angry and disappointed that we let our relationship come to an affair.

Now, you and I can become selfish, self-centered, and judgmental and walk away. But, walking away from our relationships is not fixing the problem. The problem is not with your relationship. It is within the people who are in it.

Our life partners are in relationships with us. This suggests a need for both to get help! We need to see a professional. We need to find God. We need to get back on track. We need to get help ourselves. Our life partners need to get help for themselves. It is when we are able to do that, that the possibility to reconcile with our spouse will be successful.

When I think of the deep wounds caused by my behavior, I get remorseful about the journey because it is going to take a long process to heal us.

Life Lesson

The life lesson I got from this day was that deep wounds will override your heart, especially when a person has taken you for granted. My advice for you is to leave the relationship if you are not ready to deal with the reality that your wife or husband loves you but is not in love with you. However, if you were man or woman enough to cause some of the damage, you should be willing to help clean up some of the mess.

Chapter 4
Day 4-Life Lesson 4
Evaluating the Damage

This day was my true day of redemption. When I got the chance to finally sit down with my wife and see my wife's chronology of my toxic behavior, I raised my hands, I closed my eyes, and I truly was able to express my emotions. I repented.

I told God how sorry I was. I told her how sorry I was. I no longer wanted to live a lie. I felt free. I cannot describe it. The joy that came in my heart was so peaceful and encouraging. This is the day I understood. I realized this was not about her and her affair. This was about God getting my attention. He was answering my prayers.

Just two weeks prior, I had asked God to help me become faithful to my wife. On May 31, 2014, I prayed and asked him to help me with the same thing again. The Bible says that they who hunger and thirst after righteousness will be filled (Matt. 5:16). I am so glad for this emotional pain because it helped me accept my part and role in the process of the affair and get the help that I needed.

Life Lesson

Here are the life lessons I got from my Day 4. The first lesson I received was that sometimes the answers to our problems and dysfunctions come through situations that match behavior we exhibited in our past. It's like we are getting a taste of our own medicine.

It's amazing how being home by myself now helped me to understand my wife's cry for my time and attention. Second, when you identify your answers, it's time to move forward. Finally, I realized that I needed to get help. I no longer needed to focus on my wife and our relationship. I needed to be focused on me and the help I needed to get my life back on track.

The Answer Never Appears the Way You Think

Man, I thought I was going to wake up on my Day 1, and everything was going to be great. I was not going to have any problems with my wife being onboard about the change I needed. But God had a different plan.

The plan God had for me was like getting catfished. Catfishing occurs when a person assumes the identity of someone and uses it on a social network site like Facebook, Twitter, or Instagram or on a dating site like POF, Woosk, Tinder, etc. In essence, the person pretends to be someone he or she is not. God catfished me!

I see it this way because I had chosen my change path. I had in my view what I was going to get at the end of my change. I was excited. I was ready to meet it. But when that time came, it was like this didn't look like the change I was asking for. God had already chosen it for me. His change was on His terms and in His time. It was different. It was emotionally painful. It was ugly! It was unattractive. It was not sexy. It was at this moment I realized that the prayers I prayed the day before were being answered differently than I expected. And His path to change was totally different than mine—really different. The Bible says that as high as the heavens are from the earth, so are God's ways from ours (Isa. 55:9).

This is where you probably are. I was there. It's a shock. It messes up your plans totally. I was like, "I didn't expect this." I almost felt like I was getting pranked. I was waiting for someone to jump from behind a wall to show me where the hidden cameras were. It was not a prank. It was God coming to my rescue and answering my prayers on His terms—not on mine.

I think God did it this way to hit me beneath the surface of my desire to change. What I wanted was a surface change. What surface change suggests is that I wanted change that did not require legitimate effort. God wanted core change, and in order to get the core change, I needed to put forth some effort.

Core change is that change that works beneath the surface and attacks those areas of our hearts that we did not know existed. It's like when we do a core workout at the gym. I believe this core change was what God needed to drop His seed of "love" deep in my heart.

He did it as a farmer preparing soil to plant a seed. The initial plunge into the soil is the hardest. But as he continues to plow the soil, the digging process gets easier and easier. You might be feeling the pain of the affair now, but sooner or later the pain will get less and less. God is preparing you for growth and sustenance.

I know you can't sleep. I know you have rage, anger, fear, and confusion. This is your carnal will being plowed by God's will, and what's coming up out of you is all the selfishness and self-centeredness that is stopping your growth.

Life Lesson

We will never fulfill our fullest potential in areas of difficulty in our lives until we accept the challenge of being planted in the darkness of new soil. And after much watering and nourishment from the sun, we are able to see the incremental growth into our true selves and in the direction we were meant to go.

It's Time to Go to Work

I never wanted to deal with the issues of my marriage and my need for change because I always gravitated to a quick-fix scenario. After the affair, I wanted what was quick, fast, and easy. I wanted to skip the pain and the hard work it takes to bounce back to a healthy relationship. Word of caution, quick changes do not make for a healthy, long-term commitment.

God Wants Us with Real Change

God wanted me with "real change." Real change requires us to face our demons. The demons of selfishness, self-centeredness, and being unaware of ourselves are robbing us of who we really are. I don't know about you, but I did not desire to be disrespectful in my relationship with affairs. These demons had me ignoring the important changes I needed for myself and my marriage. Now that the affair has happened, "real change" asks us to deal with the consequence and our role in it.

It's easy to see the affair as not our fault. Here's what I am asking you to do. I am asking you to take the time out of your busy schedule to investigate yourself! Find out where your issues are. Yes, this is the time to say, "What have I done that contributed to my life partner's affair?" Here are some questions I developed for you to start your self-investigation.

Self-Investigation Evaluation:

These evaluation questions are a chance for you to sit down with your life partner and get some answers about yourself and things you can work on to improve yourself. If you don't feel comfortable with this, get with a therapist. Either way, here are some starting questions.

This needs to be set up in a neutral environment where there are at least two people who love you and are willing to be open-minded and nonjudgmental. This way you have referees who can keep the communication civil. Also, you and your life partner should create some rules of engagement. This way you do not allow emotions to run high. So, let us begin.

Question 1.

Why did you cheat on me?—This question should give you a history of things your partner tolerated from you before deciding to have the affair. Ask permission to have a pen and pad so you can follow along. Or plan a time to discuss your relationship and ask your partner to make a list of the things that led to cheating. This way you can understand and learn something about yourself. You may discover, like I did, that you were selfish and self-centered. You may discover, like I did, that you were not reliable. You may discover, like I did, how you took your wife's time and effort toward you for granted. The best view of you is going to be from your life partner.

Question 2.

What are some things that I did to suggest to you that I did not care?—This question should give you a good view of areas in your emotions to address in your life, as it did for me. This will give you tools to improve and correct behaviors for your current or next relationship. This is very serious because it speaks to your moral compass.

One of the things I strongly recommend is that you listen to the answers of your life partner with a desire to learn about yourself. It will be tempting to express anger and resentment. Here's what I suggest you do in case you run into that. I want you say:

> My life partner is God's child and deserves to be loved and cared for correctly. I did not provide a safe environment for my partner to enjoy the love and care that I know I can give, so I release (him or her) from the guilt and the shame (he or she) may be experiencing as a result of (his or her) act of infidelity. I give (her or him) the grace and the mercy of God that He gave to me through Christ.

I hope this statement will help you as it has helped me to become a patient listener.

Question 3.

Where are you emotionally?—This question will gauge for you the amount of damage your behavior has caused. Your partner was not lacking anything, really. I want you to understand that.

Your partner chose to have the affair and has to take full responsibility for his or her actions. But this question will help you understand how important your love and attention were in the life of your partner. Keep in mind, you used to fulfill him or her emotionally. For me, this helped me gauge where I went wrong and how I took my life partner for granted.

Question 4.

Can you tell me how you feel about your affair?—This will help you identify, as it did me, the things that made your partner feel special to you. This is the key question. The reason it is the key question is that it not only gives you the answers to what you took for granted, it also addresses a deeper craving that this person developed for you. The lover is just the substitute. The substitute in any environment is only there for a short time. For example, when you were in grade school and your main teacher was absent, the substitute was called to take his or her place. This is what happened in our relationships. We were absent. This affair is like the principal of your grade school calling your main teacher, trying to see when he or she would be coming back to work.

Your partner really doesn't care deeply about the lover, who is not the real aim of your life partner's intimate emotional desires. You are. Trust me! The lover is not going to be there long. In the meantime, it's time for you to educate yourself about you. And having the answers to this question will possibly give you a history and a self-check of what you started and didn't finish.

Time to Move Forward

These questions should help you finally start moving forward. You are in for a ride. Yes. You are probably having feelings of anger, fear, and anxiety—you name it. All these emotions represent the serious challenge of moving your life forward.

You are going to have to make a choice at this point. Do I change for me? Or, do I change for my life partner? Here is my recommendation. You need to change your life for you. And I hope that your change does not include continuing your relationship. However, I recommend it be focused on improving your behaviors, your sensitivity, and your belief system. You need to address these things before you can even think about trying to build a new relationship or rebuild an existing relationship.

How I View Relationships Now

I see relationships now like I view computers and their need for constant updates. I understand that had I consistently gotten updated about my relationship, I would not be divorced.

Relationship Updates

Every computer system has within its programing a function and feature that allows the computer to update the software from time to time to ensure that the user is experiencing the latest changes in the software. Well, I have found that the same thing is needed for a relationship. I have a question for you. When was the last time you checked on your relationship for daily, weekly, monthly, or even yearly updates? If you cannot answer this question, these inconsistencies will soon kill and destroy your relationship. You are possibly setting your relationship up for failure.

The Problems Inconsistent Updates Cause

What happened to us in our relationships is what happens to a computer in the real world. You remember the first computers? You don't even see them around anymore, do you? However, if you were to open the inside of an old computer, it would look almost the same as a new one. The only difference would be the outside design. So what does this have to do with the affair?

What I mean by this analogy is that we were asking our spouses to continue to love us and enjoy the state of the relationship using the old, outdated process. The inside of the computer is all of the things that process the information of the computer unit. The affair is an indication that the old, outdated process needs to be updated. Our life partners were no longer satisfied with the old process. I see this process of updating as a way to improve the functionality of a relationship the same way a software update does a computer.

How to Get Your Relationship Updated

In order to explain the process of updating a computer, I am going to use the process by which computers are updated from software companies. As I looked at the process to update computers from the software companies' standpoint, I began to see how similar it was to a relationship with communication issues.

Every so often, I have noticed that when I am connected to the Internet and I shut my computer down, there is a message that tells me not to turn off my computer. This message suggests that my computer is receiving updates and turning off the power can interrupt necessary software changes for my computer's functionality. I see this process as a way to communicate changes needed in our relationships.

The Updating Process

When computer software needs an update, software companies like Microsoft or Apple send it via an online or Internet connection. This process of updating computers, I think, applies to how we can update ourselves and our relationships.

The affairs happened to us because our relationships needed updates. And I see the affairs as an Internet connection like the one we get at Starbucks, or wherever an Internet connection can be received. The connection is quick, free, and available for temporary use. Anyone can connect to free Wi-Fi at Starbucks. This is similar to the way that our life partners connected to the affairs. The connection to the affairs fulfilled inward desires.

Starbucks represents a free connection. If a person does not have a connection to the Internet at home, he or she can get connected there. Well, the lover is like Starbucks. He or she was available because there was no love connection at home. If there is an online connection at home, there is no need to go to Starbucks. The same applies to the lover.

So, what does that say to you and me? It says that we needed a love connection at home. Would you agree that there is no connection at home? How do we get a love connection at home? But before we address this question, I would like to explore the pros and cons of getting into an affair or getting free Wi-Fi versus having an exclusive relationship or a Wi-Fi connection at home.

Free Wi-Fi Love and Relationship Pros and Cons

I took to Google and wanted to get some testimonials that would reflect the pros and cons of infidelity. What I found were people who were disconnected at home and found a "Free Love Connection," just as in our Starbucks example. They were very selfish, self-centered, and angry. Check out these testimonials from *Inside Affairs*, "How to Catch a Cheating Spouse," at http://doccool.com/the-pros-and-cons-of-having-an-affair/. This is a forum created for those who were involved in extramarital affairs. Check out "Pros of Infidelity."

The Pros of Having an Affair

From Sally M., thirty-eight: "My husband only thinks about himself when it comes to sex. We have done it probably twice in the last year, both times disappointing for me but fine for him. My lover cares about my sexual needs, and we can even talk for hours about anything. He has become both a friend and a lover. It's fantastic! We're both happy staying in each other's side lives, too—no complications, no arguments, and over ten years now."

From Josh, thirty: "Sex with my lover is amazing. She doesn't consider sex as a chore or make me feel I'm an interruption in her life, like my wife. We have wild sex, and we both know that's all each other want in the relationship! We're both married but both lacking in something that we find in each other—it's a great boost to our egos, too."

From Tamika, forty-six: "After years of having next to no companionship, it's great to have met Gary. He's sweet, loving, and we both feel so connected to each other. I find it amazing that I could click so easily with someone. I still go home to my partner, but it's nice to feel I have support from my lover when things get down at home."

From Cam, twenty-seven: "My husband's barely ever home. He is always on business trips or down at the bar with his mates. My lover makes me feel like I'm in a real relationship, without having to deal with the bills, fights, or my bad moods. I couldn't be in my marriage without him, and he says the same about me. We're basically each other's backbone."

These testimonials all sound great to a person who has settled for any type of connection. They are not happy, but they would rather have the affair because it does not cost them anything. No one said anything about how the spouse would feel if he or she discovered the infidelity. These testimonials all speak to selfishness, self-centeredness, and anger. They never speak to forgiveness. The affairs seem easy.

This sounds like the Starbucks example. What they do not realize, as I didn't, is they are getting a connection anybody can connect to. Generally, in affairs, per my experience, there is never a real connection. The only connection is physical and never spiritual and mental.

The Cons of Having an Affair

Affairs only appear on the outside to be fun, loving, and risk-free. Although many people get comfortable in the connection that an affair provides, there are always points within the scope of the affair when a person feels guilt and shame, especially when considering being caught.

What the life partner does not realize is the backlash of the risk—the pain he or she will experience after being caught.
There is never a comfortable moment. Just like at Starbucks, you are only connected for a short time. If a person had an Internet connection at home, there would be unlimited access to the Internet.

Check out these testimonials about the "Cons of Infidelity."

From Brent, fifty-two: "My wife found out I've been having an affair with a woman at work through one of my work colleagues. I didn't even know they knew about it! The woman I was with didn't want anything more than casual sex on the side of her own marriage. I've now lost my wife, my three kids, and I am left with no home. My lover doesn't want to risk being with a single person so I'm practically left alone…not to mention the financial strains from all of this. I wish I could turn back time."

From Rebecca, twenty-five: "I fell pregnant while having an affair and didn't know who the father was. With extreme racial differences, I HAD to find out who the father was. My husband left me when he found out the baby may not be his. My lover didn't want it, and it was too late to stop it. I'm now a single mother living with my parents."

From Tess, thirty-seven: "I've always found it hard having an affair. I am attached to a married man other than my husband and I desperately want to share it with someone but have to keep it to myself. I can't kiss him in public, can't talk to him on the weekends on the phone from home, nor call to ask if everything's OK when I haven't heard from him in over a week. I have to be very careful if I try to e-mail him or talk online to ensure my partner doesn't find out. Secrecy really eats away sometimes."

From Martin, forty-five: "I've always been safe when I had sex with women other than my wife, but I went bareback one night with a girl I thought I could trust and had been with for several months. She gave me an STD. It was next to impossible to make an excuse to my wife on the spot why I didn't want to have unprotected sex with her. It puts yet another strain on our marriage!"

The reality is that an affair is not worth the trouble of pursuing. It sounds great to finally get someone new to meet our emotional needs and gain a new connection. This is like going to Starbucks on a regular basis just to get a connection. It seems great, but after a while, we begin to realize the cost of the connection. We assume that the affair will offer us something better. But that is not true. It would be better to have a connection at home. The reason I did not have a connection at home is because I was speaking and disconnecting from it. This made me vulnerable for a Starbuck like need for a connection. I was speaking positively about the affair and negatively about my marriage. I think I could have spoken positively about my now ex-wife, just as I had been about my affairs. You get what you speak. If you speak negatively about your relationship, all you will get is negativity. The reverse will happen if you speak positively. This will produce the connection you need at home.

Think about it when you are at Starbucks. You have to spend money on gas to get there, and you buy a cup of coffee to sit there and get connected to something that is not protected and open to the general public. And you know you will not have privacy on the connection or in your surroundings. So the best solution is to get connected at home. At home is where you can have exclusive access to your connection to the Internet. This is what your life partner can become for you: the exclusive love connection to all the needs in your life.

You might be saying that you do not have a connection at home. You might be saying, "How do I get a connection where I feel loved and appreciated without the affair?" I recommend Jesus Christ. Get connected to Him.

He can, through the power of the Holy Spirit, connect us. And as the software companies can, He can download all the love needed to heal us and introduce us to a healthy and prosperous love relationship.

The unfortunate thing about getting an Internet connection in your home is that it will cost you something. However, the best thing about connecting yourself and your relationship to Jesus Christ is that it does not cost you anything because He purchased you and your relationship on Calvary's cross over two thousand years ago. The Bible says that while we were in sin, Christ died (Rom. 5:8).

This Is Why Communication Is So Important

Connecting our relationship with Jesus Christ will give us the ability to take the necessary steps to get acquainted with God's love. This is what was stopping the communication between my wife and me. Communication was the major issue of my relationship.

It was a major issue because I did not know how to start. You might be asking, "How do I start?" This is where counseling and therapy come in. You start with getting counseling. This does not make you crazy.

I have come to see that mental health is just as important as physical health. Developing my mental health has given me tools for communicating with my family and friends my true feelings about things.

Counseling gave me the updates needed to function from a personal perspective. From the counseling and therapy, I have learned to use the information as a way to start communicating within a relationship.

Chapter 5
Day 5-Life Lesson 5
Refocus Your Motives and Your Efforts

I know you want to understand and fix your relationship. However, I didn't realize then—but I realize now—that I was trying all the same tactics that led my wife and me to living in a totally toxic relationship. I was trying to do the same things. Stop buying gifts. You are wasting money. Stop trying to win her sympathy. On this day, I realized that I just needed to let her go.

So, I am telling you to just let him or her go. You are doing more harm than good trying to convince your partner with logic. Your partner is not in love with you anymore. He or she loves you, but he or she is not in love with you. Before your partner says it to you, I figured I would say it to you. I am sure it will be said if it hasn't been already.

Here is where your focus should be. Your focus should be on you. Yes, you. I had to do it, and every person who got through this has had to refocus. Let me put it like this—you have a problem in your life. The problem requires you to refocus your attention on you and your behavior. It's time to do some soul-searching because refocusing your motives and efforts requires you and me to do some deep soul-searching.

How to Start the Process of Soul Searching

How do I start the process? I am glad you asked. I have found that this moment should be treated like a new construction site. The scenario is that the building of the last relationship was not all that great. Had it been, obviously, I would still be married. But I have identified that my relationship failed because of the deep-seated issues of my past and the belief system I developed from it. This suggests that the information I got from my father and mother about securing a healthy relationship was seriously faulty. My father and mother represent my foundation of a wholesome relationship. I did not realize then that I was my father in my relationship. But I got the blessing of my wife leaving me. I wish my mother could have done that. She was so sweet. But her sweetness was buried beneath the pain of feeling locked into a relationship where there were thirteen children. She endured unhappiness and verbal, mental, and physical abuse just for me. But at the same time, I was learning how to be enabled. My mother should have left my father in the '60s. But it was a different time. She taught me that it was OK for a man to treat a woman like a punching bag. I am saying this because she allowed my father to treat her that way. She deserved better! But God had to get me here. I am grateful. I want to encourage every woman reading this book to seek *better*. I pray you do not settle. Do as my wife did—*leave*. Hopefully, when you leave, he can find the help he needs.

This reflects the foundation I had for a relationship. I did not realize it, but my wife enabled me as my mother enabled my father. But I am so grateful to God that she had the courage to leave me and find the help and life she deserved.

What Type of Foundation Are You Building Your Relationship On?

I entered my relationship with a bad foundation. I came from a rigid religious background full of physical and verbal abuse. My father told us what to wear, where we could not go, and what we could and could not watch. And on top of that, I did not see a great example of a loving and healthy relationship between a man and a woman. My father and mother had roles—not love. I viewed my relationship in the same way—that is, one that had roles. I figured fulfilling my role was showing love.

My dad was a good provider. I am also a good provider. My dad handled conflict with aggression. This is the way I handle it. These are a couple of examples of how I identified the deep cracks in my belief system, which is also my foundation for building upon life. This type of belief system destroyed my relationship and was faulty.

I Had to Change My Belief System (My Foundation)

The first place I suggest you start digging deep is with your belief system, which is also your life's foundation. Jesus said that we must build our house (which is our life) on a solid foundation (Matt. 7:24–27). Working on your belief system is like laying a good foundation for building a house or a building of some kind. This is where all the changes have to take place. This was the best thing I could have ever done was change my beliefs about my role in a relationship.

Second, I suggest you find a place where you can get some spiritual guidance. This is like the framing for a building structure. The stronger you are spiritually, the better you grow from the pain and disappointment you received from the infidelity.

And finally, I started eating right and exercising. This helps provide a visual of improvement. As I was beginning to look good from working out, I began feeling good about myself. I gained confidence. Exercising and changing my diet gave me a new perspective on myself that was evolving from the inside out.

Start Psychological Therapy (Shore Up Your Foundation)

I have two words for you: Meier Clinics (www.MeierClinics.com). This is a renowned Christian psychological therapy clinic. If there isn't one in your area, find a good mental health clinic in your area. Check the reviews online and get a psychological evaluation. It's like bringing your car to the mechanic shop for a tune-up. This gave me the answers I needed to refocus my energy on me. This gave me the understanding I needed to forgive my wife for her affair. You see, this will clear the fog in your head. I wish I could have done this earlier. I probably would not be divorced from my wife—who knows. This is the gift to you that keeps giving. If you get nothing else from this book, I hope you take this advice. It is worth it. You are going to grow faster and healthier from the affair. It's like putting fertilizer on your lawn. It will grow better, greener, and nicer.

Your Mind Will Be Affected

Your mind is the first thing that is affected after an affair, at least in my experience. Once you are aware of infidelity in your relationship, it plays hard on your mental state. It did for me. Getting the psychological help you need should be your first line of defense. Getting help psychologically is like laying down a foundation to a building before building a structure on top of it. If you are trying to build on your old belief systems, it will not work. Building on your old belief system is like building on sand. You need something more solid to build your next relationship on.

What Are You Building Your Foundation On?

What are you building your foundation on? You can build it on something solid or something not solid like sand. If you decide to build on sand, it will not be stable. Your foundation will shift easily. I hope you desire stability in your next relationship. Your relationship needs a better place. I know mine needed it. What we need is a solid rock. Jesus gives this example in the gospel according to Matthew. He said if we build on sand the winds will blow and beat on the house, and the house will fall (Matt. 7:24–27). Is this what happened to our relationships? I think it did.

We did not have a solid foundation in our relationships. This is the reason we are in the situation we are. If our relationships had been solid, they would not have failed.

What should we do? What should we do to find a solid foundation for our new relationships? Whether you are going to be with your current partner or not, it is time to accept your losses and prepare to move forward. It's time to get solid mentally. This is your solid rock.

Why Is the Foundation So Important?

Why is the foundation so important? Jesus said winds will blow and beat upon the house. The wind He is talking about is the wind of life—that is, the hard times and challenges that life brings to us—emotional or physical pain, stress, fear, and anxiety.

Our behaviors and actions after infidelity speak to the quality of the foundations that our relationships were built on. The results of our personal lives are based on the foundations. And based on the results of my marriage, mine was built on sand. The thing we need to do now is to find a more stable building platform. Jesus recommended a rock. Because when we build our relationship on a solid rock, the winds will blow, but the house will stand the tests the storms of life can bring.

I Have Seen My Share of Storms

I am from New Orleans, Louisiana. I have seen my share of storm damage. And when it comes to homes and buildings, the well-built structures receive damage that can be repaired, and the ones that are not well built are unrepairable. This is what psychological therapy can possibly do for you. It can give you the solid foundation needed to withstand the turbulent winds of life's storms to sustain damage you can repair. You cannot repair a relationship built on sand. The blessing through it all is that you are still alive and breathing. That means that the affair did not destroy you. So it is time to count your losses. I hope you accept that you will find love again. Hopefully you will build it on a solid foundation.

Start Spiritual Therapy (Your Pillars of Strength)

What is spiritual therapy, you might be asking. Well, let me explain. Spiritual therapy for me was anything that gave me inner strength to think differently about the infidelity and the direction of my life. It can be a motivational speaker, music, art, a place, or a person. The power of this therapy is that it gives you vision and hope. The reason it gives you vision and hope is that as your spiritual resources feed your inner spirit, you will be able to see beyond the infidelity. This is what it did for me. It's like the warmth of a blanket on a cold winter day. It covers you, and it keeps you warm.

Spiritual therapy gave me the ability to see past my emotional pains, fears, and anxieties. The Bible says that without a vision the people will perish (Prov. 28:19). I had to be able to visualize a better way of living for me. I was tired of the lifestyle I had led for the last twenty years. I wanted something better. I wanted something more concrete. I wanted to change, and being able to see God coming to my rescue as a result of my lack of spiritual resources was awesome.

I hate that the act of infidelity was required to get me to change. It is hurtful. When it happened, I was not thinking about God. I wanted to kick, scream, cry, and holler at my wife for bringing that into my life. It clouded my vision. This is the importance of having a spiritual connection. It brought me inner peace regardless of how chaotic life was around me.

God Has More for Your Life

God has more for you. Life has more for you. But you and I have to see it. It is very depressing when you can't see how you are going to make it. My wife and I were together for twenty years, so I did not know what to do. I took her for granted. She is now serious about her decision to move on with her life. I remember saying to her, "You aren't going anywhere," but when she experienced something new, she was gone. To hear my wife speak about another man as if he were her savior from me was like hearing a bad diagnosis from a doctor.

We all have seen movies, been in a hospital, or been with someone who has heard bad news about a loved one's death or sickness. The emotion that is expressed in that moment is heartbreaking. The deep groans of the emotions put those of us who see it in a place where in some cases we cannot speak. All we can do is weep and mourn. I was groaning.

I am so grateful for my church. I am a member of the Potter's House. When I heard my pastor, Bishop T. D. Jakes, speak, it give me life. I purchased every sermon after that service. I would listen to them for days and months in my van or car. These words would keep me. I began to listen to positive music. I began to listen to different music genres based on my emotions. For example, I would listen to smooth jazz to relax, and I would listen to gospel to lift my spirit. I would take trips. I went to Canada. I drove to Niagara Falls. When I saw it, God speaking to me, and He said,

"Son, you have to become like the waters of Niagara Falls; they flow regardless of rain, storms, or snow." I felt God was showing me that I needed to keep moving regardless of life challenges that came my way.

In this moment, I began to see past my pain. I began to accept my pain. I began to see that all behavior has consequences. I now believe that this is the language of God. It is God's way of getting our attention, giving us a way out, and teaching us why we need to change. Signs for change for me appeared a long time ago. It was hard to change. I never wanted a divorce, but my behavior produced a divorce. The things I was doing equaled a divorce just as if you added one plus one. It would equal two. This is why your infidelity moment is more than a mistake. It is what will happen in my next relationship if I do not heed the warnings and signs of God. The divorce is the answer to my behavior in my marriage.

This is why I stress spiritual therapy. You and I need to work on our lives in a regimented and routine way. This is something I apply to my life every day now. I have found that the more I feed my inner spirit, the more my vision is secured. I can sing the words of Jimmy Cliff's song "I Can See Clearly Now (The Rain Is Gone)." This book is a part of my strength. I became a writer from infidelity. What will you have the strength to become? Life is not over. You will find love again. You will be loved again. Trust God. Trust yourself. You are not alone. I have been there. I had to learn to live in the now. Your past does not define you. Your present does. If this pain does not make you stop your behavior, then you are going to remain the same and experience the same results.

Start Physical Therapy (Structure of Beauty)

I am an event photographer. When I became aware of my wife's infidelity, I was 283 pounds. I was covering an event at a nightclub. While taking photos there, I was hurting. I got tired of being so overweight. I saw this guy who I knew to be a bodybuilder. I asked him a question about losing weight. I believe God used him that day to say to me, "Man, it is easy...It's not about lifting weights...What are you putting in your body? If you eat better and work out less, you are going to get the results you deserve." I was amazed. It stuck with me like glue to a broken teacup.

I Found What Worked for Me

I researched eating and good diets. I researched eating different types of healthy foods. Then I discovered a diet that worked well with my body. As I found the diet, I lose six pounds a week. My body changed. I began to understand that I could look better. I was recently studying the verse of scripture that says our body is the temple of the Holy Ghost (1 Cor. 6:19). I believe the temple that the writer in this verse of scripture is referring to is the temple of Solomon. Although there are other temples where God's Spirit dwelled, I believe that Solomon's temple represents the kind that God desired. In fact, David asked God to build a temple for His glory, and God refused David. God used Solomon to build His temple. Solomon was able to build it the way God wanted it. The Bible says that the temple was so beautiful that the queen of Sheba was overwhelmed by its beauty and fainted (1 Kings 10:4).

Since our body is God's temple, we should beautify it as Solomon did. Are you making it elegant and beautiful? When believed this concept of what my body represents, I began to follow a strict diet and exercise differently. God can use you and me in any way He wants. I believe God wants to be represented in excellence. I desire my body to be a structure of beauty. I had to make a tough decision. Many people who see me suggest that I look better now than I looked when they thought that I was OK. They were basing their perceptions on the money I was making. Although I believe real beauty is inward, transforming both the inside and outside of your body is what God desires.

I want to reflect His glory as the sun reflects its light to the earth. It warms us, gives us light, and causes growth. This is what I want my body to do. I want people to see me as engaging and kind. I want my body to reflect God's ray of love. I also want to be a light to those who sit in the darkness of infidelity. I want to show them that there is life after infidelity. Life is not over. You will get past this. And why not get past it looking and feeling better than you did before? This is why eating and exercise on a regular basis are important to me. I will not let this destroy me. We are giving this pain too much power. It's time that we fight back. Keep in mind we are not fighting our exes or life partners. We are fighting against the old, destructive system that caused the infidelity. What better way to relieve the stress and become healthier and stronger? This way we can stay in the fight with our focus on a better lifestyle. Make those who see you faint at the wisdom and beauty God can produce out of pain as the queen of Sheba did at Solomon's temple.

My Diet:

Breakfast:
English muffin
2 eggs
1 slice of cheese
2 strips of turkey bacon

Snack: (any fruit or vegetable)

Lunch:
chicken or fish salad

Snack: (any fruit or vegetable)

Dinner:
Chicken or fish
(any green vegetable)

My Workout: (twenty minutes)

100 push-ups
50 curls
50 triceps dips
50 crunches
100 squats
1-hour cardio (Wednesdays)

This is the diet and workout that helped me lose six pounds a week.

Chapter 6
Day 6-Life Lesson 6
God Has You Where He Wants You

This is a Friday. I am empty. This used to be the night that I was in the club "making that money." My wife hated Thursdays, Fridays, and Saturdays. My day would start at 5:00 p.m. and would last until around 3:00 a.m. At the time of the affair, I lost a nightclub account, so I was no longer working in the clubs, and I had nothing but time on my hands. This goes to show you how deceived I was. Where was the money now? You see, you and I got caught up in ourselves and forgot about the most important thing, at *home*. Now that this affair has your attention, you are right where God wants you—broken and in need of Him. God was getting my attention and answering my prayer at the same time.

My wife had left and was sleeping out. We were not separated at this time. Furthermore, being in the house with her was awkward. We walked past each other. She was gone before she ever left.

Life Lesson

Here is the lesson I got from this day. My wife was gone a long time before the affair. She wanted attention. She wanted someone to notice her smile. She wanted a sensible conversation. Guess what? She found it. When the affair was brought to light, I thought about what she now had in her life that I was not giving her.

You and I had something to do with the affair, whether you want to believe it or not. You have to decide if you want to believe that you had a role in your life partner's affair. Because if you can see where you contributed, that is a good start to understanding your partner's side. Here's why. He or she went to the other person because you failed to provide what someone else is now giving to them. The thought of your wife or husband getting needs met by someone else can be disheartening, but you have to accept that they deserve the attention and love they are getting. I have found that when you are able to do this, you will begin to experience what loving yourself feels like.

I committed myself to living a totally healthy lifestyle. I focused on making sure I was healthy mentally, spiritually, and physically. On this day, I decided that I needed a mental, spiritual, and physical makeover.

Mental Makeover

I grew up in New Orleans, Louisiana. I love my city. I love it from my core. The seafood gumbo, jambalaya, crawfish, jazz, Mardi Gras, Bourbon Street, the French Quarter—all are unique to my city. We are known all over the world for our food and our culture. But Dallas, Texas, is my home. When Hurricane Katrina hit New Orleans, my wife and I decided to make Dallas our home. There is an old saying in New Orleans about people from the projects and ghettos. We used to say, "You can take a person out of the projects, but you can't take the projects out of them." And New Orleans could not be taken out of us. We are Saints fans to the core. However, not only could you not take New Orleans out of us, you could not take the issues we battled with for years out of our marriage, either.

I Could Not Take the Infidelity out of My Relationship

This is what I think happened to me in my marriage. Although I wanted to be better a husband to my wife than my father had been to my mother, I found myself repeating the abuse. It seemed as if I did it unconsciously. I had a better education. I made more money than my father ever made. I am living in conditions far better than my father had. But it seemed that what I was trying to avoid had a place in my life. And it occupied the space undercover. This is what I was up against for twenty years of my marriage and did not recognize. This is why I am so glad for the mental makeover the Meier Clinics gave me. Meier gave me the ability to confront the issues of my past. I was able to dig deep into my past, uncover, and attack a jacked-up belief system. This belief system led me to take God out of the equation of my life. I figured I could live on my own terms. Take it from me. You can't do it on your own. Open your heart and let God in. I recommend that you find a Meier Clinic or a good place to help you with getting counseling. Trust me, you are going to be so glad you did.

Spiritual Makeover

My spiritual makeover came in the form of Christianity. The place I worship and get my spiritual work out is the Potter's House. I am open enough to understand that God works the way He wants. So, wherever you are growing and receiving the spiritual nourishment, you need to be encouraged and strengthened. This is so important. You see, I thought I could fix my life and make it what I wanted it to be. I tried to fix my situation the way I wanted to, but I soon found out that I was missing the most important solution, God. I needed God to be in control of my life. I decided to turn my life over to Him. I wanted Him to help me to know the difference between my will and His will. He was the missing piece—the missing peace I needed. Hopefully your journey now will include God. Don't leave God out! #THEMISSINGPEACEOFLIFE

The Danger of Handling Things Your Way

There is a story in the Bible about Cain and Abel. It is a very familiar story, where Cain kills Abel, his brother, in a heated rage of anger. The story introduces Cain and Abel bringing an offering of their first fruit to the Lord. The Bible states that the "Lord had respect unto Abel's offering."

Consequently, Cain's offering was disrespected or unacceptable to the Lord. Cain was angry. The Bible says that the Lord said to Cain, "Why are you wroth (angry) and why is your countenance fallen?" The Lord said to Cain that if he did well or as well as his brother, Abel, his offering would have been received or accepted. But he could not shake his anger, and he killed his brother. I read this story and found a hidden message.

The Hidden Message

The hidden message is in what has been accepted. The Lord was

50

just saying something is missing. The thing that was missing was one of Abel's lambs. I wondered what would have happened if Cain had added the lamb to his next sacrifice. You see, what the Lord was telling Cain was to observe his brother, Abel's, offering and add one of his lambs to his offering. God wanted to accept what Cain offered. But it required the addition of the lamb. But Cain took matters into his own hands and missed the blessings of God because he wouldn't add the lamb to his offering.

But we don't have to do what Cain did. The Bible says that Jesus Christ was the Lamb of God that was slain before the foundation of the world (John 1:29; Rev. 13:8). He was the perfect sacrifice. This is what I am saying to you: add Jesus to your life and relationships. Ask Jesus Christ to come into your life, your relationships, your home, your job, etc. I believe that God went out of His way to get your attention through the infidelity to bring you into His divine love, care, and purpose. I believe He is asking you and me to add the lamb to our lives.

Physical Makeover

Man, this is a very important piece of the puzzle. You have to get healthy from the inside out. Your body is God's temple (1 Cor. 6:19–20). I recommend that you start eating right and exercising. A good diet and exercise program will kick-start your body to reshape it into the person you always were. This helped with my confidence and with how I viewed myself. When you are feeling good, looking good, and doing well, I have found that you will attract good to you.

Our Physique Is Not What Drove Our Life Partners Away

Let me say that our life partners did not have an affair because of our physiques. They chose the affair as a way to get what was missing from their relationship with us. However, we must be humble enough to accept that although our life partners had affairs, they were pissed at you and me for not paying them any attention. I know it hurts. You need a motivator right now.

Your life partner's affair may have killed your view of you. I recommend that you start upgrading the old you to the 2.0 version. It is time to get rid of the old you. This is why exercise was a great help to me. I started seeing the results, and the rest is history. This will boost your confidence. It is also a really good stress reliever. I lost sixty pounds in four months. I know you can do it, too, especially for the stress relief alone. You may not be there yet, but one of the things that my new outside physique gave me is a new view of how I can continue to look if I can continue to put forth efforts toward positive changes.

Chapter 7
Day 7-Life Lesson 7
God Is Giving You a New Start

The house was empty. There was still furniture and all the stuff in the house, but I was alone now. It's amazing how "stuff" doesn't matter when you are alone. I think in a real sense God was telling me, "Welcome to her world." The silence was excruciating. It was really painful to my emotions. It is like you're moving but suspended in the air. I can understand when the Bible says that it was not good for "Adam to be alone" (Gen. 2:18). I think I know why. Loneliness will talk to you in a way that makes sense to your pain, but it is not good for your life. Although it gave me the reality check I needed to get myself together, it was hard to endure. However, the pain was necessary, and it made sense. Pain is the start I believe God gave me to the new path of my life's journey. I see pain as the necessary indicator that a change is needed. The only way pain can be avoided is to heed the warning signs.

Pain Will Get Your Attention like None Other

Without the emotional pain from the affair, this book would not exist. However, being alone strips us of the benefit of sharing who we are with the person who deserves to celebrate life with us. This is what I believe happened in my relationship. Having someone to support us plays a very important role in our successes. I think this was what my wife was looking for. She was alone. I was making money. I was buying her expensive gifts. But I was not there. I abandoned her. I left her every chance I got, as I would say, "To make that money." But when God allowed me to see life from her side on this day, I truly grasped the weight of what she had been carrying.

Life Lesson

This was the day of my newfound love and respect for my wife. Weeks later I told her how strong she was and to let me know whatever I could do to support her during this time. Here are the life lessons God gave me through this time. First, I had left my responsibility to my family and home. So he allowed me to experience—and I am still experiencing—the effects of that. Second, he allowed me to see my wife from a position of strength instead of a position of weakness. Finally, he gave me a desire to know Him again. He showed me on this day that He was always there. He revealed to me that He was there like a patient father behind his growing baby learning to walk. He was there to catch me if I fell. And He did.

I Had Left My Responsibility to My Family and Home

I thought making money, buying my wife expensive gifts, and taking her to expensive restaurants was showing her that I loved her. But when I look back on our life together, I realize that I neglected her. I left her to fight life alone. I was blinded. I was lost. You never know the importance of family until it is gone. It is easy to get caught up with money and power. It's a dangerous combination.

How I Left My Family Responsibility

A man's responsibility to his family is to be a provider and a protector. That is, he should be the source of resources. This comes with a lot of focus and commitment. He is the "house band." This is where we get the term "husband." He surrounds the family and home. I can honestly say that I was a good provider, but I was not a good protector. I brought money home, but I made my wife feel like a roommate and not a wife who was loved by her husband. I did not provide protective love.

I was very resentful toward my wife because I felt she should have been helping me with my business. I did not give her a choice. I wanted her to be with me, but what she wanted was companionship outside work. I did not see that. This is where the affair came in. It replaced the desire to rely on what was unavailable in my home. The bond was broken. I did not even notice it. It was because I was living through selfishness and self-centeredness.

The selfishness and self-centeredness blinded me. It had me believing that I was OK. It had me resenting my wife. I was not getting this or that. Or, I was not being taken care of; it was all I-I-I-I.

Life Lesson

The lesson I learned in this moment was that selfishness and self-centeredness will give you an excuse to leave areas of your responsibility that your family depends on. A man or woman who is hungry will not turn down food. In the same way, a person desiring your time and attention will not turn it down. My wife was hungry for my time and affection. I was trying to give her working with me in my business. Our families needed us to respond to the call, but we failed. This is the reason that we are in the situation we are. Now you and I have to be responsible enough to live with the consequences of our actions.

God Allowed Me to See My Wife's Strength

On this day, I lay in my bed in a fetal position. My head was on the pile of pillows I normally sleep on. They were slanted on an angle. The lights were off, and I was listening to the silence. This was painful. I could hear the cracks from the walls that she complained about. Being in my home alone, it finally hit me what she had been going through. She had done this for about four years. I thought about how strong she was. I developed a newfound respect for her and for what she went through. She should have left me a long time ago. I was not a support to her fears.

Our spouses were truly relying on us for the support needed to make them feel protected within the bounds of our love and affection. This is what our wives or husbands needed. We are what our life partners desired. We are the true comfort they were seeking. The affairs were the solutions to the emotional pain the relationships inflected on our spouses. They were asking for our love and affection, and we basically ignored them.

Life Lesson

The lesson I learned from this was that when a spouse is crying out for time and attention, give your time and attention immediately. Don't give excuses. Don't take him or her for granted. A relationship is for the purpose of relating to our loneliness together. Giving our life partners reliable love and attention will lead to deeper intimate responses from them.

My wife went through four years in this state of unreliable intimacy. This is incredible strength. This alone gave me a new view of my wife's affair. She did her best to wait for me, but I was caught up in my world. Our life partners deserved someone in their lives who could have given them the proper love. I was giving my wife the love of my earthly father. The love of my earthly father was full of abuse and selfishness. The proper love—the love that works—I have found in this season of my life is the love of our heavenly Father. She needed God's love. God's love is full of grace and mercy. What I mean by saying God's love is full of grace is that He knows that we are human and are prone to mistakes. What I mean by God's love is full of mercy is that God's love is not judgmental. God's love excuses our mistakes and sees our needs. When I understood this, I recognized that this is the only and true way to give love to someone. This is the best example of the type of love we and our life partners deserved and deserve now.

He Gave Me a Desire to Know Him Again

God was trying to get our attention long before the affair. He was not only answering our spouses' intimate desires, He was also trying to get our attention. This affair definitely got my attention. But what I am enjoying about all this is my newfound relationship with the Lord. I am at a place where I understand God's grace. I am able to love myself through grace and mercy. I never felt this good about my relationship with the Lord.

It hurt me to know my wife was being intimate with another man. But this gave me a desire to turn to God and get psychological therapy that was long overdue. I will be forever grateful for this moment. I am going to church again and wanting to be there. I am praying more. I know that God is the answer. All of what you are going through is a cry for the love of God. Can you imagine where our relationships would be if we had loved our spouses like God loves them? How does God love? God loves like a husband who truly cares about protecting and providing for his family. Hopefully you and your spouse can work this moment out. I recommend you get this relationship out of your hands. It's time to put it in the hands of God. Think about it. Our relationship is in the condition it is in because we lost sight of what was really important. Hopefully, if you and your spouse can reconcile or you find love somewhere else, you will find God and put Him first.

Chapter 8
Life Lessons Recap

The Setup—Life has a way of showing you who is in control. As I was making lots of money, driving nice cars, having a staff, and having some level of social power, I thought I was in control. I was "The Man!" I was the "Nino Brown" of my New Jack City. In the movie *New Jack City*, actor Wesley Snipes plays an inner-city drug lord who rose to the top of the illegal drug industry from the street; that was me. The difference is that my business was legal. I felt like I had arrived. God can interrupt. I did not realize that all this played to my warped perception of life and the unfulfilled needs I had. God planned all this to get my attention and to get me the help I needed.

Day 1-Lesson 1: "Listening Loud and Clear"—From this experience, I definitely know that there is a difference between hearing and listening. If there were ever a clear voice of God, I got it on this day. God allowed me to listen to what He was listening to from my wife. It was "loud," and it was "clear." Hopefully you learned to become a better listener of your spouse from this chapter. I hope this chapter humbles you. When I was able to listen, I was then able to understand my wife's cry for my love and attention in a deeper way.

Day 2-Lesson 2: "The Boost I Needed for Change"—As I look back on this day, my main focus was my need to change. Initially, I wanted to change for my wife. And you might be feeling the same way. And while I know that this might sound harsh, this affair really is about you. It's about how selfish and self-centered you are. If you are thinking about leaving your wife, husband, girlfriend, or boyfriend because of the affair, this shows just how selfish and self-centered you really are. I know it showed me. I hoped to give you a boost in this chapter to make a change for you and your future. This way you get the help and don't perpetuate the negative behavior that led to the demise of your relationship.

Day 3-Lesson 3: "Tables Have Finally Turned"—This was the day of reckoning for me. If I ever got a glimpse of my wife's loneliness and where it led her, it was on this day. The life lesson this day taught me that I never knew the extent of my wife's pain until I had experienced it for myself. I hope to have encouraged you to think about all the days your life partner was crying out to you for time, attention, and love, and the feelings he or she perhaps experienced. This way you can start making adjustments to protect your partner and affirm him or her. Hopefully this lesson will help you become a better responder to your life partner's desire for your love and attention. This was the reason you and your life partner committed to each other in the first place.

Day 4-Lesson 4: "Evaluating the Damage"—Jesus says that before a man can build, he or she must first count up the cost. This day was when my "I want to fix this and make this right" moment surfaced. Jesus's wisdom regarding building is also applicable to assessing a situation for damage control. I hope to have helped you answer some very important questions. Hopefully answering these questions will help you navigate from that pain of the affair to the clarity you need to move forward in your life. I hope the list of questions gave you some direction in evaluating the extent of the damage in your relationship. Here is a recap:

1. Have you assessed the damage?
2. Should you consider repairing the relationship you have or rebuilding a brand-new one?
3. Do you have access to the investments needed to support the repair or rebuilding process?

Whichever way you answer these questions, you put yourself and life partner in the affair in a win-win situation.

Day 5-Lesson 5: "Refocus Your Motives and Efforts"—By Day 5, I was so focused on not losing my wife and viewing her affair as a major problem that I overlooked seeing the "pink elephant" in the room. What was the pink elephant? The pink elephant in the room was me and my selfish, self-centered behavior. I figured on this day that it was easier to fix the relationship than work on myself. I did not want to admit that I had a problem. When you and I see the pink elephant in our lives, we will see the ugliness of our selfishness and self-centeredness. We will see the role they play and have played in the destruction of our relationship. This life lesson gave me a chance to see clearly the big, fat pink elephant that was sitting in my relationship. And interestingly, it looked like me.

Day 6-Lesson 6: "God Has You Where He Wants You"—If I ever prayed and cried out to God, it was on this day. It was Saturday, June 6, 2014. I was depressed and confused. I was not eating. I felt so empty. I would not wish a day like this on my worst enemy. It was brutal! I truly understand the saying "You don't know how good the water is until the well runs dry." It was like being in the desert in one-hundred-plus-degree weather and seeing a pool of water. But when I go to dip my hand in it, I find that it was a mirage. As I look back on this day, God had me where He wanted me. He wanted me to be in a position where I was totally dependent on Him to survive. This would be the case if I were in the desert looking for water. I would definitely need someone to save me if I were to survive. This is the point where I realized how far I had gotten away from God. I don't know what your interpretation of God is, but this lesson certainly gave me a new view of Him and His desire for my life.

Day 7-Lesson 7: "God Is Giving You a New Start"—Day 7 was an awesome day for me. I did several things on this day that I hadn't done in a while. On this day, I paid my tithes to the church. I hadn't done this is years. I got to church before it started. It was a new feeling about my life. On this day, I was really focused on finding my way. I incorporated a new word into my vocabulary: *journey*. The life lesson I got on this day was that every new start comes with new problems to confront. We have to learn to confront those things and not ignore them. Over time, we ignore issues and challenges, only to confront something in our lives that we should have confronted years ago.

Thanks for your support. I hope you were blessed. I want you to know that there is a light at the end of every tunnel. However, in the tunnel of life, I pray you seek the light that is in Jesus Christ. Love you!

THE BLESSING OF INFIDELITY

61

Bonus Chapter

Chapter 9
Two Ways the Devil Can Steal Your Relationship

In thinking about ways the devil could steal from me, I thought of two ways a person could steal from me. The two ways I felt related most to a relationship are robbery and burglary. I would like to use these two ways to talk about how a relationship can be stolen. First, I want to discuss the robbery scenario and then the burglary one. What I found in looking at these two ways was the way the devil got into my relationship.

Scenario One: Robbery

The first way the devil can steal from me is by robbing me. Robbery is a direct approach that inflicts fear on its victims, which discourages them from putting up a fight. Most robbers have a dangerous weapon to aid in stealing from their victims. The weapon can be a knife, a gun, or a blunt object. The weapon is to suggest to the victims that physical harm will be inflicted on them if they do not cooperate with the robber. In essence, the robber uses fear against his or her victims to have them cooperate with his or her demands. When I consider if the devil robbed me of my relationship, I realize that the devil did not use this tactic to infiltrate my relationship because it was not a direct approach and there was not any fear involved. So I ruled out robbery.

Scenario Two: Burglary

The second way the devil can steal from me is by burglarizing my home, car, or office. In my experience, when a person's house, car, or office is burglarized, he or she is not aware it is happening. The burglar seeks times when his or her victims are vulnerable because he or she can burglarize victims' sacred places and go unnoticed. In this way, the burglar can make a move and steal from his or her victims when they least expect it.

I think this is the type of stealing the devil inflicts on committed relationships. This is what happened to you and me. Everything that took place in the affair happened behind our backs and when we least expected. It is believed that most burglaries are done by people who are familiar with their victims. I think our life partners fit the profile. This is what the devil did to us. He sneaked into our relationships while our jobs, success, and money preoccupied us, and he robbed us of our family.

But this form of stealing has a solution. What is needed to combat a burglary is an alarm system. Had I had an alarm system in my marriage, it would have notified me of the intruder the same way an alarm system works in a home, car, or office. I see now that just as my home needs an alarm system to protect it from intruders, every relationship needs an alarm system that protects it from relationship intruders.

Bonus Chapter

Chapter 10
How to Install an Alarm System in Your Relationship

If you are going to install an alarm system in your relationship, it must be installed the same way an alarm is installed in a car, home, or business. Every alarm system has three elements. The first element of an alarm system is the detector. This is the device that we place on the walls in our homes or businesses. The detector is what is connected to the sensors. The detector is the part of the system that causes the alarm to sound off when an area is infiltrated.

Second, every alarm system has sensors. These sensors are placed around the environment being protected to signal to the detector that an area in the environment has been infiltrated. For example, sensors are placed on windows and doors throughout a home or office. And if intrusion activates the sensors, the detector can alert and identify the area that has been infiltrated.

Finally, most alarm systems are connected to a hub. The hub is to notify us and to notify the authorities on our behalf. The hub notifies the authorities and us because an area of our home or office was entered after the alarm was activated.

The Relationship Alarm Detector

A relationship alarm detector in a relationship is God. I see now that God has got to be placed on the walls of every relationship. I think we place the security of our earthly father's examples as safeguards for our relationship. But God is the best example of a loving and caring father. He is the one who can teach us and give us the lessons of love to help us secure our relationships. Just like the alarm detector detects what sensor in a home or office is going off, God shows us what things in our lives are not secure. The best thing about God is He is no different from the alarm company. ADT is not going to make us put an alarm system in our home or business. Guess what? God won't, either. He wants to be invited into our relationships. This way He can place the sensors of love and protection in places that need them the most. He wants to be like the person installing your alarm in your home. The installer explains to you how to use the alarm and where the sensors are. Allow God to show you. Ask Him for understanding for your relationship. He will detect for you what needs to be addressed.

The Relationship Alarm Sensors

The sensors are placed on windows and doors so that if the alarm is triggered after we activate it, we can identify the area that caused the alarm to sound off. For example, if you activate an alarm sensor at the front door of your home and someone enters that door, the alarm detector will identify the area entered and cause the alarm to sound off. In this same instance, I see how creating this alarm system scenario in a relationship will help protect it from intruders. I have identified several relationship sensors that will help me protect my next relationship. The first is communication, the second is provision, and the last is the sex sensor.

Communication Sensor

I see this sensor as being very important. Many times, couples place sex and provision over this sensor, but I see it as the most important. I look at it as the one placed around the front door of a home or business. It is the most avoided but most desired place of the intruder. If the intruder can come through the front door, then he or she can take things out, and no one would suspect anything. If an intruder goes through the front door undetected, it is more than likely he or she can steal and get away with most of our stuff.

You see, that's what the lovers did to us. They used communication to invade our relationships. Had we been communicating with our life partners, as we should have been, then the lovers would not have had a chance to manipulate their way into our relationships. Although I say that our life partners' affairs happened behind our backs, the intruders came into our relationships through the front door. The sad part about it is that our life partners let the intruders in.

The front door of anything unprotected poses a threat of great loss. This is what happened to us. I am divorced now, and I not only lost my relationship, but I lost my credit rating, weight, some of my drive, and much more. So, I am telling you to start the process of communication because it is critical to the next relationship.

Provision Sensor

Being able to support your life partner financially and emotionally is important. This sensor speaks to the security of knowing that your partner has your back when life sometimes hands us blows in our finances and emotions. I likened this sensor to the ones that are placed around the windows. Although anything that is taken from us can be replaced, it is still a challenge to work to get it back.

A window intrusion, as I see it, is not as bad as a door intrusion. Although any intrusion is unwanted, a person who burglarizes a home or office through a window generally does not make off with large valuables. However, it is very possible that those small valuables the burglars take can be worth a big price. These valuables can be jewelry, money, clothes, shoes, etc. So, having an alarm that can sound off when a window seal is broken protect you and me against intruders who are after our small valuables.

What are our small valuables in our relationships? A small valuable in a relationship is anything that can administer support to a life partner. Here are some things that can administer support to a relationship. Watching a movie while cuddled on the couch, walking in the park while holding hands, and having a nice dinner are all ways to administer love to your spouse. Sending an impromptu text that says, "I am thinking about you," is a good feature to this sensor. Paying a bill is a good feature to this sensor. When a potential intruder sees the security of a relationship with a provision sensor, he or she is discouraged and seeks out another victim.

The Sex Sensor

Intimacy in a relationship is important. Especially the intimacy that is associated with sex. However, sex was a challenging process for me. My view of sex was based on porn and flawed education about it. I would liken this sensor to the alarm we place on our safe that we have in our homes or offices. We seek to protect this—from not only intruders who are outside our homes but also those who are in our homes. Sex is the safe. Sex is deeply rooted in offering oneself as an expression of love. But in order to get to the expression, there is something that needs to be unlocked.

With most safes, per my experience, there is always a code to enter before a person can access it. I feel that the code to open the safe of a relationship is courtship. Courtship is the art of communicating with a man or a woman, telling him or her that you are interested. Courtship is what produces, in my experience, the desire to express intimate fancies with a life partner. So, if a man or woman is not creating courtship within a relationship, then the sexual fancy will not be addressed. Courtship absent from a relationship is like having a safe left open, exposing all our valuables. To understand courtship, I suggest that you find a book or an expert on the subject. If a man or woman won't court you, he or she is asking not to get to know you.

It's clear to me that I placed sex and provision above communication. But I have found that communication is like securing your relationship at the level of Fort Knox. Many of us suffer in silence, and we find it easy to communicate with others instead of with the ones we claim we love. Open your mouth and say something. Speak from your heart! That is what happened to me. I had discovered that the insecurity of my relationships was deeply rooted in the trauma of my past. Once I was able to get the help I deserved, I was able to navigate my way to the security of finding the help I needed. When I was able to do this, I soon realized what healthy love security looks like.

Chapter 11
How Computer Updates Relate to Starting the Communication Process in a Relationship

Whenever there is a need for a computer or software company to update its customers' computer systems, the computer companies take to the Internet and send updates. However, the settings of a computer's operating system will determine how the operating system will receive the updates. A computer system can receive updates from a computer or software company in one of two ways. The update settings are automatic and manual. Let's take a look at what the settings are and how they might relate to our relationships.

Automatic Setting in a Relationship

An automatic update is when a computer connected to the Internet is updated whenever a company sends an update. The benefit to the computer owner is that he or she does not have to monitor the computer for updates. The user assumes that the company has the best interest of the computer's operating system in mind. But what the user does not realize is that sometime the updates that are sent to an operating system can affect its operations and programing, which may open the computer up to viruses. This is what happens in our relationships when we have them set to receive automatic updates.

We become irresponsible and assume that we are getting all we need from the relationship and our partners are satisfied. However, the downfall with this thinking is that not all updates benefit a computer system. "Automatic updates" may come across as being awesome and free of responsibility, but the reality is we are allowing things into our relationships that really do not need to be allowed. This is why we complain when we get a bug from the computer companies' updates. But the real question is who is responsible? I think you get the picture. It is time that we start taking responsibility for the updates we get in our relationships. This is why I prefer to set my computer system to a manual setting.

Manual Setting in a Relationship

A manual setting in a computer operating system allows the computer user to monitor the updates and upload only the updates that the user deems necessary for a computer's operating system. This way the customer has full responsibility for all of the updates for a computer system. This puts the responsibility on the user and not the company to update a computer's operating system. In the same we should manually update our relationships. So, just as the company has a set time to send updates to a computer system to keep it functioning properly, so does a relationship need a time set up to keep it functioning properly.

Whichever way you are going to update and upgrade your relationship, I hope that you do it with love and respect for you, the person involved, and God.

Chapter 12
How to Set Up, Update, and Upgrade Time for Your Relationship

In order to set up update time for your relationship, it is important for both parties in the relationship to see this as a vital piece for keeping the relationship intact. Both have to believe that the relationship should have update time.

What Is Update Time?

Update time is when life partners sit down in an environment where they can't be interrupted and discuss where they are mentally, physically, and spiritually in their relationship. This is like the question posed on Facebook and other social network pages, "What's your status?" The way you answer can be critical to persons in your network identifying how you are feeling. For example, I have seen a Facebook user putting a smiley face next to a profile with "excited" next to it. And then someone's profile may have a frowning face with "sad" next to it. This tells us how that person may be feeling. Just as in this example, update time lets our partner know our "status."

The update time has to be viewed as a time to get updated about the health of your relationship. Do you know the status of your relationship? This is why update time is so important. As in the example of software companies like IBM, Apple, and Microsoft sending updates to consumers' operating systems, it is relative to update time. When a company sends updates to a consumer's computer, what does that mean?

Why are companies spending so much money on web engineers and system supports? Why don't they allow the bug or virus in your system to stay there? You want to know my answer to this? Well, I am going to give it to you anyway. They want you to be happy. Yes, happy!

One more question: Where does the information to fix the

issues with the consumer's computer operating system come from? You guessed right—the "consumers"! So, just as the computer companies want to make their customers happy with the use of their computers and software, I see how I should have taken the same approach with my relationship. But in order to do that, I must be willing to do the following:

1. **Set Up Update Time:** This must be taken seriously. Your friends and family cannot interrupt this time. This must be put on your calendar in a way that reflects how often you and your life partner would like to focus on dealing with issues in your relationship.

2. **Have Tools Available to Assist in Communication:** The best way I see to communicate is to have the following things available:
   A. **Pen/Tablet/Smartphone**
   B. **Paper**
   C. **Calendar**

   This way, your life partner and you can communicate effectively and have something to look back on for future conversations. I think this type of communication should be taken seriously. Just as the computer companies want to correct issues with their operating systems for consumers, I feel we should have update time to correct issues within our relationships.

3. **Have a Place for Your Updates:** I think the best places for updates are places that create relaxation, fun, and peacefulness. For example, you could set up a date with your life partner to have picnic in a park. Or you could get some nice wine, sit on your candlelit patio, and discuss your relationship. Or you could cook dinner and talk at the dinner table. Just make sure this place speaks to creating an environment that really helps support flow and tranquility.

4. **Have Some Questions You Need Answers to Available:** Having questions your partner can support answering for you is important. I pray that you be as genuine as possible. What I mean is that you should ask your partner in a way that does not sound like you are trying to one-up him or her. The questions should support bringing peace and support to your life partner.

Questions for Starters

I recommend that you create some questions that you want to know about.

Here is a list that you can start with:
1. **How are you feeling about our relationship?**
2. **What are some things that you have identified that you feel we can improve?**
3. **Give me three words that describe your feelings for me.**
4. **Do I make you feel attractive and wanted? If not, what do you imagine a husband should be doing to make his wife feel attractive and wanted?**
5. **Am I giving you enough attention?**
6. **Do you feel lonely? If so, tell me in what ways.**
7. **Do you feel like you can talk to me about anything? What are some things that you feel you cannot talk to me about?**
8. **What's important to you in a relationship now compared to our past?**
9. **How do I make you feel when we are intimate? What are some of your fancies and desires? What are some areas where I can make improvements?**
10. **Do you ever feel like I take you for granted? If so, tell me how.**

These starting questions will help you gauge the status of your relationship. I also recommend you connect with a marriage counselor therapeutically. This will be a way to get the help you and your partner need. It's so easy to go out and just get into another relationship. We all must deal with and confront the issues. It can be done before we leave a relationship or after. It is proven that we have to deal with it. Computer companies deal with customers' problems before they go out and buy another company's computer and operating system. The idea is that companies want to make consumers happy because they know that they are up against some fierce competition. They also know that the other companies don't care about what happens to their company if they lose customers to them. The same thing applies in a relationship. If we are not making our life partners happy, they become vulnerable to outside people. This is why communication is so important.

When we are able to update ourselves in a relationship, we are able to build and develop a wholesome and healthy relationship.

Sometimes updates from computer and software companies come with recommendations for upgrades.

It Is Time to Upgrade Your Relationship

What is an upgrade? The upgrade is a feature or benefit with a new device that comes with everything that the old model did not have. Just as the computer companies recommend upgrades, so should a relationship seek to be upgraded with better features and benefits. In this way, a relationship changes and grows year after year, maintaining its freshness. Do you feel that your relationship is due for an upgrade? Would you like to know more about how to upgrade your relationship? Here is how you can start!

When an upgrade is brought to market, it is promoted, as Samsung does with its slogan "The Next Best Thing Is Here!" What does it mean to have an upgrade? Having an upgrade means things are going to flow better than they did with the old model. It means that the manufacturer has listened to the customer and has improved the features and benefits of a device. For example, one feature for a computer or smartphone can be that the device now can download information faster. This way, the consumer can share information faster and more easily than with the previous model. Ultimately, an upgrade is a feature or benefit that speaks to the needs of consumers about a particular product. I think that is needed in the same way in a relationship.

Just like companies upgrade features to devices and products, persons in a relationship should be looking to upgrade themselves as part of the relationship. When we upgrade ourselves, we are aspiring to become better people. That is, we are looking to improve on a feature of our lives and determine how we and those who support us can benefit from it. When was the last time you supported your life partner's dream? Has your life partner ever expressed a desire to go back to school? When was the last time you asked about your life partner's business? This is what was needed with our relationships. The people we were with may have been growing professionally without us.

At some point in our relationships, we experienced incredible communication. But as time went on, we failed to keep improving ourselves. Imagine using a computer for years without connecting it to the Internet so that it could receive the necessary updates it needed to run properly. What do you think is going to happen when you finally connect that computer to an Internet connection? Have you ever tried to shut down your laptop and had to wait for the updates? Based on my experience, a computer that has never been updated by being consistently connected to the Internet will take a longer time to get caught up with updates to function properly than one that is connected. It can take, in some cases, days before the computer can be used again.

This is what happened in our relationship. The affair was the message that it was time for an update. But when we finally got the news of the affair, represented by the Internet, we finally realized that we were missing a great number of updates. So instead of our partners getting frustrated and crying out to us for a better relationship, they got tempted, as we all do, with "The Next Best Thing." The lover is no different than you. But he or she represents perhaps new features, functions, and usability. The lover may represent an upgrade. But with every upgrade sometimes comes problems.

The Main Problem with Upgrades

Although the lover may represent an upgrade, I want you to know, as I noticed with my partner, that she may really still be in love with you, the old model. Here's the thing about the old model. The old model needs to be upgraded. I want you to try to control yourself. Just like anything, once a person gets anything new, he or she is excited for some time. But as soon as the person gets used to it, he or she realizes that the old model was just as good. You represent the familiar. The lover represents a new journey. Let him or her have the journey. Don't try to control the person. You focus on you. Focus on your physical, spiritual, and mental health. Upgrades do not always mean that the new model is "The Next Best Thing"! If that were so, why are companies coming up with "new and improved" over and over? Once the thrill is gone, the partner will finally realize what he or she has done and will try to come running back. This is why you need to stay focused on your mental, spiritual, and physical health, as I did. I want you to know that the grass is not always greener on the other side of an affair. And I think eventually your life partner will realize that. This is why refocusing your motives is important. This way, when the life partner returns, he or she can see that you have grown and have moved on separately. You are perfecting and progressing, not stressing and reflecting. However, if you want to continue in your relationship and you are willing to create times for updates with your partner, then knowing how to recommend upgrades for your relationship is important.